NORDSTROM GUIDE TO MEN'S EVERYDAY DRESSING

NORDSTROM GUIDE TO MEN'S EVERYDAY DRESSING

by Tom Julian

CHRONICLE BOOKS
SAN FRANCISCO

WRITING THIS BOOK ABOUT SPORTSWEAR INTRODUCED ME TO A MORE CASUAL MEN'S STYLE SENSIBILITY THAT EXISTS WITHIN NORDSTROM. THIS EXPERIENCE WAS INDEED AS REMARKABLE AS WRITING MY FIRST BOOK. IT WAS A GREAT JOURNEY LEARNING HOW SPORTSWEAR HAS TRANSCENDED FROM JUST LEISURE WEAR TO WHAT WE NOW CALL "EVERYDAY DRESSING." I WANT TO THANK ALL THE TALENTED AND PASSIONATE SALESPEOPLE AND MANAGEMENT TEAMS, INCLUDING JEFFREY KALINSKY, THAT MADE THIS IMPORTANT ASPECT OF DRESSING COME TO LIFE. I COULD NOT HAVE DONE IT WITHOUT YOU.

–TOM JULIAN

Published exclusively for Nordstrom by Chronicle Books LLC.

Text © 2010 by Nordstrom, Inc.
Photographs © 2010 by David Peterson.
Illustrations © 2010 by Jonas Bergstrand, Söderberg Agentur.

ISBN 978-0-8118-7262-1

Manufactured in China.

Fashion Photographer: David Peterson
Digital Technician: Mark Gordon
Fashion Stylist: Tim Teehan
Product Stylist: Stacey DuCharme
Illustrator: Jonas Bergstrand, Söderberg Agentur
Color Separations: Imagine Color Service, imaginecs.com

10 9 8 7 6 5 4 3 2 1

Chronicle Books LLC
680 Second Street
San Francisco, CA 94107

www.chroniclebooks.com/custom

CONTENTS

AH, SPORTSWEAR. NOW THERE'S A CONCEPT A GUY CAN SETTLE INTO. THAT EASY WORLD FILLED WITH EVERYTHING FROM PANTS AND SWEATERS TO SPORT SHIRTS AND JACKETS IS AS WELCOMING AS IT IS INFORMAL. BUT SPORTSWEAR IS NOT EXACTLY A NO-BRAINER. DRESSING CASUALLY CAN REQUIRE MORE THOUGHT THAN WEARING A SUIT.

As a global trend analyst and men's style expert, I watched the early nineties with fascination as sportswear became a part of our wardrobe seven days a week. Corporations that were once tailored suiting stalwarts embraced the idea of casual dressing, allowing for a relaxed work environment that many believe resulted in increased productivity. All of a sudden the golf shirt had a life off the links, khakis went double-duty, and sport coats no longer required a button-down and necktie. But many men told me that they were confused by suddenly having so many options. We all know the rules when it comes to wearing a suit, but what about dressing casually?

Forget the rules. Think occasions. As you'll discover in this book, the six essentials of everyday dressing include the iconic sport shirt, sweater, pants, shorts, jeans, and jacket. The choices you make in your sportswear wardrobe are best guided by the casual and dress occasions in your everyday life.

Nordstrom has been known for quality, classic menswear ever since it first began selling men's apparel in the sixties. Throughout each decade, this specialty store has helped generations of men navigate the murky waters of dressing for every facet of their lives. Until recently, the balance of a man's professional attire was composed primarily of formal items such as suits, ties, and dress shirts. But now that most of us dress more casually more often, the contents of men's closets are mirroring that trend. Today there are as many sportswear options as there are places to wear them.

Which pieces of sportswear you pull from your closet on any given day depends entirely on one thing: where you're going. On the following pages are the four most common occasions you'll encounter: workday, after hours, weekend, and travel.

DRESSING FOR SUCCESS TODAY MEANS SOMETHING DIFFERENT FROM WHAT IT USED TO. NO LONGER DOES "WORKING" MEAN SHOWING UP AT A CORPORATE OFFICE MONDAY THROUGH FRIDAY, WITH THE OBJECTIVE OF BLENDING INTO A SEA OF SUITS.

Today, our work environments encourage us to express our individual point of view. There's something to be said for standing out from the crowd in high-quality pieces you can combine effortlessly. An easygoing button-down in light blue gingham—or another classic cotton pattern—goes with everything and (this is the best part) can even be laundered at home. Chinos in khaki, grey, and even brown or black look and feel comfortable in almost any workplace and come in a broad variety of fits and styles. When temperatures dip, wool pants—grey pinstripe is a classic—carry all the sophistication of a suit, with none of the fuss. Finish the look with a button-down shirt and classic patterned tie. When a sport coat is not required, opt for a black leather jacket, knit polo-style sweater and slip-on loafers. Either option makes a modern statement in the workplace.

WHEN THE SUN GOES DOWN, MAKE LIKE CLARK KENT AND CHANGE FROM THE CLOTHES THAT SIGNIFY YOUR EVERYDAY GRIND INTO SOMETHING THAT FEELS MORE LIKE YOU.

Whether you're hanging with old friends in the neighborhood or hoping to meet someone new downtown at the latest hot spot, you want to combine your favorite go-to classics with something current that really makes a statement. While most clubs these days don't require more than a basic outfit, when have you ever wanted to be a part of the least common denominator?

Even though it's not required, why not make your night-out look all about your jacket? Think in terms of the three easy pieces: the shirt, the pants, and the jacket. Then focus on contemporary fabrics and trim silhouettes. For example, top off your wash-and-wear cotton shirt and well-worn dark denim jeans with a nylon motorcycle jacket that shows you're in the know. If it's too warm for a jacket, opt for a signature shirt as outerwear. Whether you go Hawaiian or preppy, consider layering your shirt over a T-shirt and pairing with jeans or pants to express your personal style. Dress for a great time and you're sure to have one.

WITH THE NUMBER OF ACTIVITIES MOST OF US HAVE PLANNED, SOMETIMES THE WEEKEND CAN FEEL LIKE A SECOND WORKWEEK. WITH CHORES, SPORTS ACTIVITIES, AND SOCIAL OUTINGS, YOU WANT TO DRESS FOR COMFORT AND MOBILITY—WITHOUT LOSING YOUR SARTORIAL SELF-RESPECT. (THIS MEANS IT IS NOT OKAY TO LIVE IN GYM CLOTHES, UNLESS YOU'RE SPENDING THE ENTIRE WEEKEND AT THE GYM.)

Your foolproof formula? The track jacket can actually be a source of style and not too casual. Mix in iconic pieces, from a polo-style shirt to a pair of easy-fit jeans, according to the weather. In the summertime, a graphic tee plus a pair of soft, washed shorts that seem like they've been in your wardrobe for years will take you wherever the day does. Slip on some rugged flip-flops and a canvas belt, and you'll have achieved that unstudied ease usually possessed only by those who vacation for a living. When the days grow short and the weather chills, layers will become your best friends. Piling on the pieces—like a T-shirt under a cashmere pullover under a down vest—gives a man a wealth of options when he's going back and forth between indoors and out.

WHILE WE ALL LIVE DIFFERENTLY FROM ONE ANOTHER, ONE THING IS THE SAME NO MATTER WHO YOU ARE: WE HAVE NO CHOICE BUT TO LIVE ON THE GO. THIS MAY MEAN TRAVELING OVERNIGHT TO TOKYO—OR DISNEYWORLD. LOTS OF TIME IN THE CAR—OR ON THE SUBWAY.

What's key to the process of coming and going? Multitasking pieces that give you function as well as comfort. You know that guy, the one you see breezing through the airport in crisp pants and a blazer, instead of warm-ups and a baseball cap? How many times have you silently wished you looked like him? I'm launching a one-man campaign to bring the dignity back to travel. An unstructured blazer with corduroy details, paired with pants that won't wrinkle, has all the comfort of jeans and a T-shirt, but promises to imbue your look with old-school cool. When it comes to comfort, your footwear options are boundless, from easy-on, easy-off driving mocs to canvas sneakers.

THE SIZING OF CASUAL CLOTHES CAN BE DIFFICULT TO DECIPHER. SOME ITEMS RUN FROM S TO XXL; OTHERS ARE NUMBERED, BUT OFTEN INCONSISTENTLY. CHECK OUT THE DIAGRAM AT RIGHT TO DISCOVER YOUR BODY TYPE, THEN READ THE RECOMMENDATIONS THAT HAVE BEEN TAILORED JUST FOR YOU.

Throughout this book, you'll find fit tips aimed at your particular silhouette. Understanding your body type will help you hone in on the choices that truly make the best out of what you've got. The natural friendly fit of sportswear allows you to be more relaxed when choosing your pieces.

ATHLETIC

Just as achieving an exceptional build calls for a little bit of work, selecting clothes that suit you may require a little extra attention, but it's worth it. Look for contemporary fits—and don't be afraid of the word "stretch." It doesn't mean an item will be tight—just that it will spring back into shape after each wearing.

BROAD

You've got a bigger physique, so choose clothing that fits: neither too tight nor too baggy. Darker pieces with vertical lines or patterns help as well. Avoid anything labeled "skinny," "low-rise," "cropped," or "shrunken."

LANKY

If you're lean and tall, you're used to serious gapping at the cuff and sleeve. Choose items labeled "long," "tall," or "extra-long," and befriend a tailor who will provide just the right nips and tucks.

COMPACT

If you top out at 5' 6" or less, think unified color and streamlined belts that match your trousers—anything that won't divide your body into separate territories. You'll do well to stock up on T-shirts and knits which come in "fitted" and "trim" options.

A SIMPLE OUTFIT ALWAYS STARTS WITH A SHIRT, PANTS, AND A JACKET—REMEMBER THE THREE EASY PIECES. IF YOUR PANTS OR JACKET REALLY STAND OUT, SOMETHING IS ASKEW. BY AND LARGE, IT'S YOUR SHIRT THAT WILL CARRY THE DAY. AFTER ALL, THINK ABOUT HOW MANY TIMES YOU'VE BEEN ABLE TO CHANGE YOUR OUTLOOK JUST BY PUTTING ON YOUR "LUCKY" SHIRT.

SPORT SHIRTS CAN BE DESCRIBED EITHER AS "WOVEN" OR "KNIT." WOVEN FABRIC IS MADE ON A LOOM; KNIT FABRIC IS JOINED TOGETHER BY A SERIES OF LOOPS.

Because of the manner in which it's produced, woven fabric typically lacks elasticity—think of the tight snap of a shoeshine rag. Woven fabric also holds its shape, so it projects a more tailored look. Roll up your sleeves and they stay rolled up. Iron your collar and it stays stiff. Since a cotton shirt made from woven fabric sits away from the body, allowing air to circulate, it keeps you cool. And it looks cool, too.

Knit fabric has some give-and-take to it—that's why you can get your head through a crewneck sweater. Wovens and knits are like ketchup and mustard—singular on their own, sometimes even better together.

Knit fabrics tend to fit easily, hang well, and are not prone to wrinkling. Perhaps most important, a knit item "breathes" and absorbs moisture—hence athletic-inspired shirts are made of knit fabrics. Active occasions usually call for knits.

Both knits and wovens have a strong presence in the well-rounded closet. Read on to find out which styles and silhouettes are right for you.

STYLE TIP
Knits are what you wear to the football game;
wovens are what you put on to meet the parents.

WITH AS MANY KINDS OF SPORT SHIRTS AS THERE ARE SPORTS, THERE'S SOMETHING FOR EVERYONE. WHETHER YOU'RE THE KIND OF GUY WHO LIKES TO HIT THE LINKS OR LIVES IN CUFF LINKS, HERE ARE A FEW GREAT OPTIONS.

POLO-STYLE

With its soft-knit collar and three-button half placket, the cotton piqué polo-style shirt is timeless and versatile. Dressed up or dressed down, a polo-style shirt's enduring functionality will never go out of style.

T-SHIRT

Made of thin-knit cotton and available in both crew and V-necks, tees don't wrinkle and have enough give to suit every body type. That's why most of us can't live without them.

V-NECK

A neckline for the guy who doesn't want to feel restricted, the V-neck will also stay well hidden under a button-down. Just be sure not to go too low, or you'll seem stuck in the seventies.

HENLEY

Basically a collarless polo-style shirt with long sleeves, the henley is ideal when temps just begin to dip. It can be found in a variety of weights and silhouettes.

CAMP

When the weather is hot, this short-sleeved shirt with a notched collar, straight hem, and loose body—often made of understated silk, sometimes in a fun print—is oh-so-cool.

NOVELTY

This shirt is a work of art—and sure to be a topic of conversation. It's often distinguished by a contrast between its collar, cuffs, and body, a signature print, or unusual buttons.

BUTTON-DOWN OXFORD

Constructed like a dress shirt—with single-needle tailoring and durable buttons—this is the classic cotton shirt for all seasons and a wardrobe essential whether you're dressing up or down.

MILITARY

With flap pockets, a bold placket, and a streamlined silhouette, this shirt's distinguishing features can be straight or shirttail hems, epaulets at the shoulder, or a rolled sleeve that buttons with a tab.

fabric

WHILE THERE ARE SCORES OF VARIATIONS, WHAT MOST CASUAL FABRICS HAVE IN COMMON IS NATURAL FIBERS AND EASE OF CARE. WHETHER YOUR SHIRT IS MADE OF SOFT COTTON JERSEY OR NUBBY OXFORD CLOTH, YOU WANT TO BE ABLE TO THROW IT ON JUST OUT OF THE DRYER AND LOOK EFFORTLESSLY PUT-TOGETHER.

SOLID YARN DYE

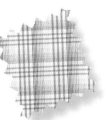

SMALL CHECKERBOARD

BOLD NOVEL STRIPE

VINTAGE STRIPE

GINGHAM CHECK

COTTON PIQUÉ

COTTON SLUB

NYLON PERFORATED

DID YOU KNOW?
The T-shirt was born when central heating called for a lighter alternative to long johns.

BECAUSE THEIR SILHOUETTES ARE PRETTY STRAIGHTFORWARD, SPORT SHIRTS DERIVE MOST OF THEIR PERSONALITY FROM SEEMINGLY IMPERCEPTIBLE DETAILS THAT MAKE A SURPRISING IMPACT. JUST IMAGINE YOUR FAVORITE KNIT SHIRT WITHOUT ITS SIGNATURE LOGO, OR YOUR BUTTON-DOWN IF IT DIDN'T, WELL, BUTTON DOWN.

ACTIVE ACCENTS
From perforations to grommets, many of the details that give a T-shirt or a polo-style shirt its signature style derive from athletic inspiration.

CONTRAST STITCHING
When thread decides to stand out instead of blend in, the result is sporty and bold.

ROLLED CUFF WITH BUTTON TAB
The weekend long-sleeved shirt becomes short-sleeved once the cuffs are rolled and pushed up and the tab is buttoned.

UNIQUE PLACKET
Whether it's a contrasting color or a hidden pattern, a unique placket makes a shirt fun—but not too much fun.

BUTTON-DOWN COLLAR
Developed to keep athletes' collars down during sporting events, the presence of these buttons is a surefire way to distinguish a casual woven shirt from a dressier one.

POCKET
Whether it's a flap, a patch, or a western, a breast pocket adds interest—perfect for storing your slim tech toys.

CUFFS
Casual shirts will normally sport a single button for a relaxed, looser fit. A French cuff adds a twist on the classic, often found in contrasting fabrics with detachable fasteners.

NOVELTY BUTTONS
Whether they stand out because of contrasting color, innovative shape, or vibrant thread, out-of-the-ordinary buttons give a simple shirt flair and personality.

TRAVEL TIP:
To avoid wrinkles, ask your dry cleaner to fold your shirts with tissue for packing.

WORKDAY DRESSY
For a formal day at a casual workplace, or a casual day at a formal one, try pairing a blue and grey checked shirt with grey wool trousers. Brown shoes, instead of black, add sophistication.

WORKDAY CASUAL
When you're really ready to roll up those sleeves, a short-sleeved polo-style shirt paired with khaki pants lets you get down to business in cool comfort.

AFTER HOURS CASUAL
How do you add a little edge to your favorite solid-colored shirt? Pair it with colored jeans, some sporty kicks, and you'll be ready to run around town in style.

AFTER HOURS DRESSY
Throw a tailored vest on over a workday shirt and you've got a cutting-edge—yet classic—nighttime option. The black accents on this blue and grey combo make it perfect for an evening out.

WEEKEND CASUAL

Layering a long-sleeved T-shirt under a short-sleeved polo-style shirt shows your fashion confidence, and boat shoes display personality. The weekend is the time to have fun with your clothing.

WEEKEND DRESSY

Few things feel as good going on as a washed poplin shirt—it's as cool and smooth as freshly laundered sheets. Along with a white tee and linen-blend pants, it forms an outfit that's put-together without trying too hard.

TRAVEL CASUAL

Choose a polo-style shirt with a contrast collar when you want a sporty look. Round out the athletic vibe by pairing your jeans with trainers, and you're ready to sprint the length of the terminal to catch that plane.

TRAVEL DRESSY

The only reason anyone might suspect you're wearing a wrinkle-free shirt is that, even after endless hours in transit, you look freshly pressed. This striped Nordstrom Smartcare shirt is a man-on-the-go's best friend.

Fitting casual pants seems pretty straightforward to me, but I'm never quite sure how a laid-back shirt is supposed to fit.
It can be hard to find the perfect fit in casual shirts since they are not sized according to neck measurements like dress shirts are. And because there's so much variation between the *S*'s, *M*'s, and *L*'s of different brands, it's crucial to try even the easiest-looking shirts on. That said, a tailor can certainly help you get things right. He or she will look at three key areas: the width between shoulder seams, the length of sleeves, and the shape of the body. Shoulder seams should hit right at the broadest point of your shoulder. Side seams can be taken in to remove extra fabric (but never from the center back). Rather than shortening long sleeves on sport shirts, try wearing your cuffs rolled or open.

I am an active guy, and I tend to perspire a lot—even outside the gym. I have no choice but to wear a button-down to work, but how do I avoid overheating?
Performance fabrics are not just for running gear. Today's technology allows for moisture-wicking, cooling materials to be used in sportswear, so you're getting all the comfort of an activewear piece with all the polish of something much more refined. The fibers in the fabric are specially designed to lure perspiration away from your bod and into the shirt, keeping you calm, cool, and collected.

I've seen the word "performance" on tags for activewear, but what does it mean when applied to clothing I don't plan to work out in?
Performance fabric is the technical term for cloth woven to accomplish a specific task—say, wick moisture away from the body when you're running in eighty-degree heat (a jersey you'll find in the athletic department), or stay looking pressed when you're running a meeting of eighty colleagues (a Nordstrom Smartcare sport shirt). It's a prime example of making technology work for you.

STYLE TIP:
If there were only two shirts left on earth—the blue oxford and the white piqué polo-style shirt—the world would still be a very stylish place indeed. Like a good red wine, these two pieces go with everything and get better with age.

SWEATERS: THEY'RE NOT JUST FOR WINTER ANYMORE. GOOD SWEATERS ARE SOCIABLE AND SUITABLE FOR LAYERING, OR FOR ADDING A BIT OF TEXTURE AND COLOR TO AN OUTFIT. THEY CAN BE BULKY AND WARM IN RICH YARNS OR AS LIGHT AS A COTTON SHIRT IN LUXURIOUS TWO-PLY CASHMERE.

LIKE YOUR BEST CHILDHOOD BUDDY, SWEATERS GROW UP WITH YOU. FROM THAT ANCIENT PULLOVER YOU STOLE FROM YOUR GRANDFATHER IN HIGH SCHOOL TO THE CARDIGAN YOU JUST CAN'T SEEM TO TAKE OFF LONG ENOUGH TO SEND TO THE CLEANERS, YOUR GO-TO SWEATER IS ALWAYS AROUND WHEN YOU NEED IT. SWEATERS ARE SO VERSATILE TODAY THAT YOU CAN ALMOST WEAR THEM IN LIEU OF A JACKET. OF COURSE, WHEN IT GETS CHILLY, YOU CAN ALWAYS LAYER A JACKET ON TOP.

CREW NECK
Whether paired with a button-down or T-shirt, the crew neck is a real outfit builder. Sporting a finished collarless neckline, most styles have a rib-knit cuff and waistband for comfort.

CARDIGAN
All cardigans share in common a button or zip front, but there the commonality ends. Formfitting or loose, in light- or heavyweight yarns, the cardigan is as versatile as any casual jacket (and immune to wrinkles).

POLO-STYLE

It should come as no surprise that the popular polo-style shirt has been adapted into a sweater. Often knit of fine-gauge luxury yarn, this style is worn dressier than its counterpart.

V-NECK

A V-shaped neckline reveals the T-shirt or button-down you've layered underneath. For those who don't want the restriction of being "buttoned up," this becomes the go-to style for comfort.

VEST

Flat or cabled, the sweater vest is an underutilized but indispensable everyday staple. Built to maintain your upper torso core temperature without encumbering the arms, the sweater vest gives plenty of play to a good-looking shirt.

TURTLENECK

This layering piece is distinct with a high, close-fitting collar that is often rolled or turned down. Slim versions look great by themselves or even with a suit, while the avid skier might prefer a bulkier version.

HOODIE

Taking this classic, sporty shape from the active world into the realm of sweaters dresses it up without compromising utility or comfort. It's usually designed with a full front zipper, side entry pockets, and drawstring hood.

HALF-ZIP

Designed with a stand-up collar to be worn open or zipped, this style provides versatility. Pair it with a shirt and tie for business or throw it on over a T-shirt on the weekends.

yarns

COTTON
Cotton is a nearly perfect fiber. It's light, usually washable, and ideal for warmer climes.

WOOL
The most classic of sweater yarns, wool has a crimp that allows it to trap heat and gives it bulk.

CASHMERE
Made from ultrafine goat's hair, this yarn produces a lightweight yet cozy and soft garment.

COTTON-CASHMERE BLEND
The perfect choice for the man who wants it all—the softness of cashmere, with the body of cotton. It's ideal for warm spring days.

CASHMERE-SILK BLEND
These natural fibers combine to create a luxurious knit that offers lightweight warmth with a slight sheen.

MAN-MADE BLEND
A man-made blend—of viscose, nylon, and acrylic, for example—feels great and is often a great value.

A GREAT SWEATER IS AN INVESTMENT THAT YOU'LL ENJOY FOR A LONG TIME TO COME. TO MAKE THE RIGHT CHOICE, IT'S WORTH YOUR TIME TO LEARN SOME BASIC TERMINOLOGY.

GAUGE
Think knitted stitches per inch. Gauge varies according to the size of the yarn and needle. Big needles and heavy yarn might produce a 3 gg (the abbreviation for gauge) sweater, while a 16 gg sweater, accordingly, is very fine and light. Just remember: the higher the number, the finer the knit.

RIBBED
By reversing the stitch, knitting machines create a vertical valley, or rib, in the knit. Ribbing strengthens a sweater and, of course, adds interesting texture. Just be sure a ribbed sweater glides over your torso rather than clings to it.

HEATHER
A heathered fabric is produced when different colors of yarn are knit together, producing a variegated appearance. This approach creates a unique finish that is a softer alternative to basic solids.

RAGLAN SLEEVE
Two diagonal seams connect these sleeves directly to the collar. This construction maximizes an athletic physique, which may be why you'll find it on baseball shirts and jackets.

BANDED CUFFS AND BOTTOM
Meant to be worn untucked, this finishing technique prevents the hem of a sweater from fraying and keeps your silhouette classic.

PLACKET
Whether it's full- or half-length, connected with buttons or a zipper, this midline split at the neck is what distinguishes a cardigan or polo-style shirt from a crew- or V-neck pullover.

CABLE KNIT
Cable knit refers to a knitting technique that gives a sweater texture and built-in pattern. A cable-knit sweater is a piece that works for both ultra-casual and a bit dressier occasions.

ELBOW PATCH
A small piece of leather or suede on the elbow originated as a way to save table leaners from holes, but it now makes a subtle style statement. Rugged but sophisticated, the elbow patch is a nod to classic, collegiate style.

WORKDAY DRESSY

There's just something so effortless about a V-neck sweater worn with a button-down and trousers. It's a look that's been looking good for almost a century, and it suits everyone between the ages of 8 and 108.

WORKDAY CASUAL

A double-zip cardigan is as easy to wear—and as indispensable—as your favorite sweatshirt. Except no one will think you're on your way to the gym.

AFTER HOURS CASUAL

Cardigans aren't just for wearing over button-downs; they add a certain something when tossed over a knit. This combo strikes just the right balance between hip and classic.

AFTER HOURS DRESSY

For a chilly evening out, try layering a wool sweater under a blazer, instead of tossing on your overcoat. You'll have more control when it comes to your internal temp, and you'll look cool no matter what.

WEEKEND DRESSY

Few things feel better than a cashmere sweater. Don't be afraid of strong colors—like this rich beet red—when you really want to look smart. Accents in grey, tan, and beige—instead of black or navy—add unexpected dimension.

WEEKEND CASUAL

You can toss a half-zip over your graphic T-shirt for warmth and a touch of polish, whether you're on your way out the door for a busy day of errands or just on your way to the living room for a movie marathon.

TRAVEL DRESSY

If you want the perfect travel uniform, this is it: monochromatic grey in the form of a heathered zip sweater and Nordstrom Smartcare trousers. This combo will have you on your way in style.

TRAVEL CASUAL

The beauty of a double-zip hoodie is that it stays fastened in the middle while giving you all the room you need at the top— and bottom. This one even has a hood, which is why it's perfect for the modern globe-trotter who may encounter unexpected weather.

Can a sweater be altered?
A sweater is one of the rare items best left untouched by the hands of a tailor. With natural wear, a sweater will shape-shift to fit your body, like a pair of jeans.

What's the best way to store my sweaters?
You may think you're doing your sweaters a favor when you leave them on hangers, in dry-cleaning bags, until you wear them next. This is not the case. It's important to remove them from the hanger and the bag as soon as you get them home. Sweaters need to be exposed to the air, and folded, not hung, so they don't lose their shape.

I've always wanted a cashmere sweater, but I'll admit the price has made me gun-shy. I want to invest in something I can wear forever.
The miracle of cashmere is that it manages to be both warm and light at the same time. So let your cashmere sweater do what it does best and choose a fine gauge that will work as a layering piece for all four seasons and in a range of climates. Scottish cashmere is the gold standard. Choose a simple pullover silhouette in either a crew- or V-neck (whichever you prefer) and in a neutral color such as black, navy, camel, or heather grey.

What's the best sweater to purchase so I can wash and go?
Cotton blended with a little nylon helps a sweater retain its shape after washing—and is often a great value.

STYLE TIP:
Don't be afraid to let your favorite sweater add interest to an outfit in an unexpected way. You can layer a fine-gauge hoodie under a blazer, or wear a cashmere pullover as a stylish alternative to a sweatshirt.

THOSE ETERNALLY COMMUTING BETWEEN THE CONFINES OF SUIT SLACKS AND THE OPEN SPACES OF JEANS ARE ABOUT TO DISCOVER A NEW MIDDLE GROUND IN A WIDE ARRAY OF CASUAL PANTS. THE WEALTH OF OPTIONS AVAILABLE WILL HAVE YOU FEELING COMFORTABLE AND LOOKING APPROPRIATE WHEREVER YOUR DAY TAKES YOU.

PLEATED CHINOS

A small dart at the waist that allows for more fabric through the body, the pleat was invented to be accommodating. These harmless little gathers have become less popular, but there's nothing like pleats for a man seeking comfort.

Best for: All body types

FLAT-FRONT CHINOS

There's a reason chinos make up part of almost every uniform, official and otherwise—they're classic, neutral, and made of cotton twill. With a waistband that hits squarely at the waist and relaxed leg openings, chinos are truly democratic.

Best for: All body types

FIVE-POCKET PANTS

Born of the jean, five-pocket pants have the same essential features—watch pocket, doubled seams, rear patch pockets, slim fit—without the rivets. Whether in twill, denim, or corduroy, think of them as jeans-lite.

Best for: Compact, Lanky

UTILITY PANTS

From cargo to carpenter, some of our most enduring styles have been time-tested on the job. Throw on a pair of pants covered in pockets, and you're ready for anything. Cargo pockets come in various shapes and sizes, making them appropriate for almost all occasions, but try not to overload them.

Best for: Broad, Athletic

CORDUROY PANTS

With a style and ease inspired by jeans, but with a bit more polish, cords with a relaxed fit can be worn year-round. Just choose a thinner wale (the vertical lines woven into cord fabric) for spring/summer, and a wider one for fall/winter.

Best for: All body types

WOOL PANTS

Whatever their details—on-seam pockets, a self-tab waist—wool trousers have a certain panache. Look for a pair in super 100s performance wool.

Best for: All body types

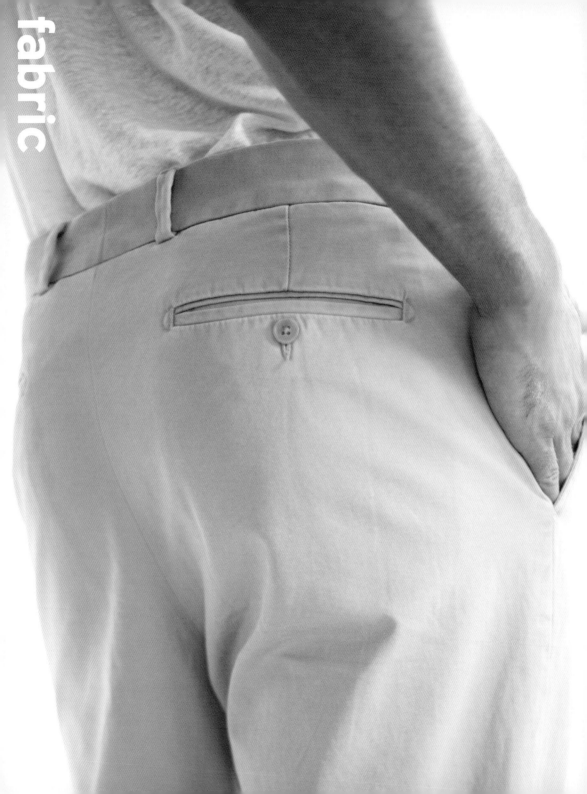
fabric

THE RIGHT FABRIC FOR YOU AND YOUR CHOSEN OCCASION HAS TO LOOK GOOD, WEAR WELL, AND FEEL GREAT. WITH SUCH A TALL ORDER, IT'S A GOOD THING MEN HAVE PLENTY OF OPTIONS.

COTTON   COTTON TWILL   CORDUROY

LINEN   WOOL   NYLON

DID YOU KNOW?
There seems to be an eternal debate over when to call neutral cotton pants "khakis" or "chinos." "Chino" originally referred to a fabric and "khaki" to a color, but whichever term you use, don't worry—in modern usage they're synonymous.

PANTS BASICALLY ALL FUNCTION THE SAME WAY ACROSS THE BOARD. BUT GREAT DETAILING, WHETHER OBVIOUS OR SUBTLE, IS WHAT REALLY GIVES QUALITY PANTS A LEG UP.

COIN POCKET
Five-pocket styles seem somehow bare without a coin pocket. Designed to separate your coins from your keys, it's located on your right-hand side just below the belt loop of your trousers.

CONTRASTING INTERIOR WAISTBAND
This secret luxury lets you know your trousers are a cut above the rest, indicating that they've been handcrafted with high-quality workmanship. And it adds grip, helping to keep your shirt tucked in.

SNAP/BUTTON CLOSURE
Adding a casual, functional touch, buttons and snaps fasten quickly, hold like crazy, and are, well, snappier than a hidden closure.

TAB CLOSURE
This smooth operator lies flat instead of bunching up under your belt—which, incidentally, is optional with tab closures.

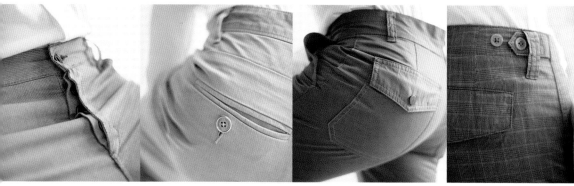

BUTTON FLY
This retro feature is easy to mend, won't catch, and is considered a sign of quality. It may be a bit slow to fasten, but a button fly stretches better than a zipper when you're seated.

BESOM POCKETS
Set in, instead of on, your pants for a streamlined appearance.

PATCH AND FLAP POCKETS
Set on, not in, for a more casual look—sometimes with flaps, as shown here.

WAIST BUTTON TABS
A long, rectangular tab, it makes the most of its space, fastening both inside and outside.

DID YOU KNOW?
There are two pairs of trousers every man should have: grey wool and khaki cotton.

WORKDAY CASUAL

Make classic chinos look sophisticated by pairing them with tonal neutrals. When accompanied by an olive green polo-style shirt and brown shoes, the khaki color of these pants becomes integral, not an afterthought.

WORKDAY DRESSY

The classic work pants—in grey wool—get an update when a bit of stretch is thrown into the mix. Add a blue and white striped button-down and a tie that brings in both blue and grey to give your look that office-appropriate edge.

AFTER HOURS DRESSY

A pair of pinstriped trousers takes on an entirely new identity when paired with a turtleneck—just as you do when you leave the office. Add a brown leather blazer and shoes in rich espresso, and you'll fit right in at downtown's newest hot spot.

AFTER HOURS CASUAL

Khaki pants, cotton knits, a lovingly beat-up belt, and desert boots will have you feeling as though you're in front of the TV in your sweats but looking smart enough for dinner and a foreign film.

TRAVEL CASUAL
There is a place for active pants beyond the gym, and that place is called a minivan. When you're going to be traveling in the trenches, choose a lightweight, pull-on style that you can move in and that you can wash easily. (New performance fabrics dry faster than a three-year-old can say, "Daddy, I spilled my grape juice!").

WEEKEND CASUAL
The key to making your thermal and sneaks go beyond the half-pipe is refined poplin cargos and a sophisticated neutral palette. This combo takes its inspiration from legions of skater dudes, yet still works for the weekend.

WEEKEND DRESSY
Pinstriped pants don't only come in wool—they're great in cotton, too. Add a cardigan, a gingham shirt, and driving mocs, and you'll resemble a country gentleman lounging around your manor—even if your manor is a third-floor walk-up.

TRAVEL DRESSY
You could tie these trousers in a knot and they'd emerge unwrinkled—that's the genius of Nordstrom Smartcare. A good thing for anyone who has to spend endless hours on a plane.

APPROACH CASUAL FOOTWEAR WITH AN EVERYDAY ATTITUDE. THINK STRIDE, WITH STYLISH CONFIDENCE. ON WEEKENDS, SELECT A DRIVING MOCCASIN, WHICH HAS BECOME THE NEW WARM-WEATHER STAPLE. FOR AN IMPROMPTU DINNER, A SOLID LOAFER REALLY DOES THE TRICK. DURING THE WORKWEEK, A PAIR OF STYLISH LACE-UPS, LEATHER SLIP-ONS, OR CHELSEA BOOTS FIT THE BILL.

WORKDAY
A lace-up oxford is a classic choice for any office environment.

AFTER HOURS
Worn with dark denim, a polished black loafer sends a sophisticated nighttime vibe.

WEEKEND
New technology means you can opt for a shoe that looks like a loafer—but feels like a sneaker.

TRAVEL
Driving moccasins are the classic choice for those in transit—but you need not be behind the wheel to wear them.

I hear different opinions on how long pants should be. What's the lowdown?
Your pants should be long enough to rest on the tops of shoes with a slight backward slant toward (but not covering) the heel of your shoe. When you've got it right, there will be a dent in the fabric at your ankle, that famous "break" you hear so much about. If it's not happening for you off the rack, here's a tip: Have it altered. Most men do.

I don't like ironing, haven't got the time, don't really want to learn how to do it. What are my options?
The day will come when half an hour before dinner with a client, you pull your pants from your suitcase and find them looking like a used tissue. No time for the dry cleaner, no obliging mom around. So learning to iron is a pressing issue. (Sorry, I couldn't resist.) In the meantime, Nordstrom Smartcare fabrics, which don't need ironing, and linen, born to look rumpled, will get you by.

No matter how carefully I hang up my pants, the hanger's locking bar dents them above the knee.
Flip them over! Store pants upside down and full length, clamping the hanger bar on the hems. Too much trouble? Drape pants over a hanger bar, preferably a thick one with a coating that prevents slippage.

I'm having a pair of machine-washable pants hemmed. Cuffs or no cuffs?
No cuffs. Natural fibers will have a longer lifespan when finished without them, because a cuff deteriorates after several washings. And when it comes to washing, wash first before altering.

I like everything about a pair of pants I just tried on, except the rise is too long. Can I have this altered?
This is probably the most important piece of information I can give you when it comes to altering pants: You cannot alter the rise (the vertical measurement from the waistband to the bottom of the zipper). This is the one area that must fit off the rack. To know whether a rise measurement is right for you, think comfort first. You should be able to move comfortably, whether standing or seated. The inseam should not make contact with your body, nor should it sit so far away that it gaps or gathers when you walk.

STYLE TIP:
If you can only buy one pair of pants per season, stay away from tissue-weight pants and go for 100-percent cotton brushed chinos, which can be worn year-round.

WHEN SHOPPING FOR SHORTS, LOOK FOR THE SAME SIGNS OF QUALITY AND STYLE AS YOU DO IN PANTS. SAVE THEM FOR LEISURE TIME AND YOU'LL BE COOL, LITERALLY AND FIGURATIVELY. I'D LIKE TO GO ON THE RECORD HERE TO SAY THAT I AM NOT A FAN OF WEARING SHORTS IN THE WORKPLACE, NO MATTER THE OUTSIDE TEMP. IN MY MIND, SHORTS ONLY WORK FOR THE WEEKEND.

THESE DAYS, WE'RE KNEE-DEEP IN A WIDE RANGE OF SHORTS STYLES, FROM CREASED TO FLAT-FRONT, FLAP POCKETS TO DRAWSTRINGS, BELOW-THE-KNEE TO MID-THIGH. SO YOU'RE BOUND TO FIND THE RIGHT PAIR OF SHORTS TO SUIT WHATEVER WARM-WEATHER OCCASION WAFTS YOUR WAY.

PLEATED TWILL
On the upside of dressed down, these trouser-cut shorts are strong and crisp.

FLAT-FRONT TWILL
A fail-safe classic, these will be your go-to garments for brunches, barbecues, and everything in between.

CARGO

Cargo shorts, loaded with hard-working details, are the perfect foil for a simple tee- or polo-style shirt.

GOLF

Golf shorts can be pleated or flat-front. And while they may look just like "regular" chinos, they're fashioned from performance fabrics that are sure to measure up to your game.

COMFORT

With a drawstring or elastic waist, these easygoing shorts are all about easygoing comfort.

RUNNING

Made of performance fabric, these breathe well and wick away moisture on long hauls.

BOARD

Inspired by surfwear, with a hallmark drawstring. If you're on the lanky side, opt for a longer length that hits just below the knee.

SWIM TRUNKS

While swimwear styles ebb and flow, roomy, mid-thigh trunks remain an essential.

fabric

ONCE YOU'VE DETERMINED THE STYLE OF SHORTS YOU NEED FOR YOUR OCCASION, MAKE SURE THE FABRIC IS EQUALLY APPROPRIATE. FROM COOL COTTON TO SPORTY MICROFIBER, THERE'S A FABRIC THAT STANDS READY TO MEET THE CHALLENGE.

WASHED LINEN
The last word in cool, linen has a slight sheen and, in this case, ventures a subtle plaid.

COTTON SEERSUCKER
Born with a crinkle that never sticks or creases, this micro-pattern offers pulled-together comfort.

LINEN-SILK BLEND
Ah, linen. Ah, silk. Lightness and crispness combined. Here's a ready combination when temperatures and humidity soar.

COTTON CANVAS
Tough and low-maintenance— now there's a friend worth having. Cotton canvas can tackle any job and will clean up great.

MICROFIBER/POLYESTER
Grandpa's leisure suits gave it a bad rap, but polyester (a.k.a. microfiber) is strong, holds its shape, and can carry off bold patterns easily.

NYLON
Exceptionally light, nylon dries quickly and has elastic qualities that provide cool comfort.

SHORTS COME WITH ALL THE FEATURES OF THEIR LONGER-LEGGED FOREBEARS—AND MORE. LIKE AMPHIBIANS, THEY'RE EQUIPPED WITH DETAILS THAT HELP THEM SUCCESSFULLY ADAPT TO ANY WARM-WEATHER EVENT.

SNAP WAISTBAND
Like paying off a mortgage, a bold snap brings security and closure.

CARGO POCKETS
Inspired by military styles, one of these large patch pockets can hold a can of soda (but that doesn't mean it should).

BUTTONS
More than simply functional, buttons at the tab closure and on pocket flaps can also make a design statement.

ELASTIC INSETS
Shy away from an elastic waistband if you are carrying extra pounds—a cinched midsection is not a good look.

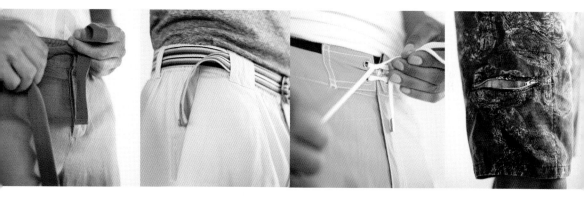

DRAWSTRINGS
Thick or thin, of a
complementary or
contrasting color, the simple
drawstring makes a style
statement while tied to an
essential job.

TUNNEL LOOPS
These superwide belt loops
are a sleek alternative to
the traditional approach.

LACE-FRONT
Surfers prefer a tie
closure because it won't
come undone even in the
gnarliest waves.

ZIPPER POCKETS
On a day you're running
around town (or just after
your kids), it's nice to know
your keys and wallet
are secure.

DID YOU KNOW?
Bermuda shorts originated with the British. Tropical London? Not exactly.
British military forces came up with the attire in the early 1900s so that
their personnel would be comfortably dressed during duty in tropical climes.

AFTER HOURS DRESSY

You may think the phrase "dressy shorts" is an oxymoron (versatile as they are, shorts simply don't work at work). But plaid linen shorts, paired with a slate blue button-down, make the grade in any resort town. Add driving mocs instead of sandals if you'll be dining out.

AFTER HOURS CASUAL

A bit more length goes a long way if you're wearing shorts after dark. Even when accompanied by a graphic tee and canvas slip-ons, these slate blue shorts are clearly a step up from what you'd don at the beach.

WEEKEND CASUAL

Your classic khaki shorts get a new lease on the summer when you add your favorite striped polo-style shirt. It's that hard-to-define, yet totally effortless, preppy cool.

TRAVEL CASUAL

Sometimes traveling can feel like a combat sport, so if you know you're in for a tough ride, opt for easy athletic separates. These track shorts have an elastic waist—perfect if you'll be visiting a drive-through or two (don't worry, we won't tell your trainer).

TRAVEL DRESSY

When it's warm but you still want to look put-together, just think of your shorts as pants. There's no reason you can't wear them with an argyle vest and a baseball jacket, especially if you're in for hours and hours of air-conditioning.

WEEKEND DRESSY

These walking shorts look crisp because of their lighter palette. There's just something cool about opting for a long-sleeve button-down with shorts—it brings them away from the pool and into the city.

THERE'S REALLY ONLY ONE RULE WHEN IT COMES TO PAIRING SHOES WITH SHORTS: YOUR SOCKS SHOULDN'T SHOW. A SPORTY SNEAKER OR ATHLETIC SHOE PARTNERS WELL WITH A NO-SHOW ANKLE SOCK. BUT IF YOU OPT FOR THE COMFORT OF A BOAT SHOE OR THE TRADITION OF A LOAFER, SOCKLESS IS THE ONLY WAY TO GO.

AFTER HOURS
Contrast stitching and a serious sole give this driving moccasin style and substance.

WEEKEND
Even if you're not planning to spend the day on deck, boat shoes provide an easy and comfortable option for knocking around in.

TRAVEL
When it comes to planes, trains, and automobiles, you want a shoe you can run in and easily slip out of. A cool sneaker does the trick. The stripe gives this one attitude.

ACTIVE
If your shorts are made of a performance fabric, pair them with athletic shoes or risk looking like a tourist.

My wife said my shorts reminded her of Chevy Chase's in *Fletch*. I don't think she was paying me a compliment. So just what is the right length?
While the mid-thigh look was a grabber in the eighties, it looks dated today. But if your shorts dangle beyond your knees, pull 'em up, Jack. Aim for the top of the knees—which for most men means a 9" inseam—a smart look that protects you from farmer tans and hot car seats.

Do I really need to belt my shorts? There's not much to hold up.
A belt can pull your look together. However, let the occasion be your guide when deciding whether to wear one. A canvas belt is a good choice for a more casual affair—you can even try one in color. While leather, wide with no sheen, will polish things up a bit. Never, ever use a dress belt on shorts! It's like pairing a baseball cap with a tuxedo jacket.

I'm a bit hard to fit—my waist is thick but my legs are skinny. Can a pair of shorts be altered?
Ultra-casual shorts styles, or those fashioned from ultra-lightweight fabric, should fit pretty well off the rack. So with swim trunks and cargos, you may have to take them as you find them. But if you've found a quality pair of golf, flat-front, or pleated shorts that need a taper or tweak, your Nordstrom tailor will be happy to shape them up.

I am traveling to the islands and the dinnertime dress code at the restaurants is "elegant resort attire." Does this mean shorts with a Hawaiian shirt?
Well . . . not really. The key word to pay attention to here is "elegant." Take it to mean, in this case, "pants."

STYLE TIP:
Top off shorts with a tee or polo-style shirt and a blouson jacket. They've been doing it on the islands for years. Save the look for off-hours, though—shorts draw too much attention to themselves at work.

JEANS ARE NOT ONLY AT HOME ON THE RANGE, THEY HAVE RANGE. WHAT OTHER PANTS CAN YOU WEAR FOR ROUGH RIDING IN THE MORNING AND FINE DINING IN THE EVENING? JEANS HAVE TRANSCENDED THEIR WORKWEAR ORIGINS TO ACHIEVE FIRST-CLASS STATUS. HOW? UPGRADES SUCH AS BETTER FIT, FINER FABRICS, AND SIGNATURE DETAILS MAKE THEM AN INDISPENSABLE STAPLE IN EVERY MAN'S WARDROBE.

STRAIGHT

This is the real McCoy, the cut that hearkens back to the original jean. No extra fabric here—straight legs fit close to the body all the way down.

Best for: Compact, Lanky

BOOT-CUT

Starting with a trim fit on the upper leg, boot-cut jeans flare below the knee to make room for boots. Givin' your boots the boot? No worries—boot-cut jeans look good with slip-ons and sneakers, too.

Best for: All body types

LOW-RISE

With a waistband that hits closer to the hip than the belly button, a low rise reveals multiludes. If you feel the impulse to pull your pants up, trust your inner critic and try a different style.

Best for: Compact, Lanky

MID-RISE

This waistband hits at your natural waist and is universally flattering to every body type.

Best for: All body types

SKINNY

With a lower waist and a slim-jim cut, these stovepipes are popular with rock 'n' rollers. Warning: It takes a pretty lanky physique to pull on—and pull off—skinny-cut jeans.

Best for: Compact, Lanky

RELAXED

With a skosh more room in the waist and thigh and a touch of taper to the leg, these are easy-fitting and great for sitting.

Best for: Broad, Athletic

THE WAY DENIM FADES AND FRAYS IS JUST PLAIN BEAUTIFUL, SO IT'S NO WONDER TEXTILE DESIGNERS HAVE CREATED A SEEMINGLY INFINITE NUMBER OF VARIATIONS ON THE DENIM THEME. BECAUSE MOST JEANS SHARE THE SAME DETAILS, FABRIC AND WASH ARE WHERE A PAIR CAN REALLY DISTINGUISH ITSELF.

CHECK OUT THESE OPTIONS:

VINTAGE DARK

CLEAN

WHISKERED

DISTRESSED

RAW

BLACK

TRAVEL TIP:
Add stretch jeans to your wardrobe. You'll appreciate the extra comfort the next time you have to sit through a six-hour flight.

JEANS: YOU KNOW 'EM WHEN YOU SEE 'EM. BUT LOOK CLOSER, AND IT'S CLEAR THAT NO TWO PAIRS ARE EXACTLY ALIKE. FROM BUTTONS TO RIVETS, IT'S THE LITTLE THINGS THAT GIVE A PAIR OF JEANS PERSONALITY.

CONTRAST STITCHING
From bar tacks (areas reinforced with zigzag or whipstitching) to triple-stitched seams (areas that have been stitched three times for strength), the common thread is strength and style.

EMBROIDERY
Whether it's a decorative detail, a logo, or that back pocket flourish that identifies a brand, denim embroidery is graphic, not delicate.

POCKETS
Every pocket on your jeans is there for a reason. But the purpose of pockets goes beyond utility—their shape and placement add character and style.

YOKE
This all-important piece of fabric above the back pockets gets your jeans to sit right on your hips for a custom fit.

RIVETS
Originally applied to provide extra strength on points of strain so that jeans could withstand days of hard labor, these little metal buttons are an authentic artifact of days gone by.

ZIP FLY
Jeans went from button to zipper as society became mechanized. The button fly has been reembraced by purists, but a zipper offers ease and still does the trick for those who have a need for speed.

BUTTON FLY
A row of buttons hidden under the fly's placket, this sturdy construction won't let you down.

BELT LOOPS
The number and thickness of belt loops varies. And sometimes—quite counterintuitively—they look best without a belt.

WORKDAY DRESSY
Dark jeans are a smarter choice for the work environment. Paired with a tie and a cardigan, they're perfect for a creative meeting on- or off-site.

WORKDAY CASUAL
When you have to roll into the office on a weekend, you don't have to wear your track pants. Soft, washed jeans paired with a gingham button-down and suede lace-ups will keep you feeling confident should you run into the boss.

AFTER HOURS DRESSY
Ah, the power of black denim. At first glance, you might not even know these are jeans, right? Black goes where blue can't, especially when paired with a velvet blazer and patent high-tops.

AFTER HOURS CASUAL
Here's what happens to black denim when it's treated to a premium wash process: It goes grey, soft, and easy. With a T-shirt and windbreaker, these jeans mean you'll look extra cool at your favorite neighborhood haunt.

WEEKEND CASUAL

Well-worn jeans have always been your go-to item for weekends. Shown here, this vintage finish looks great from Friday night pizza to Sunday afternoon football.

WEEKEND DRESSY

These dark denim jeans have a slight sheen the way some trousers do—which takes them way beyond the bounds of where your stonewashed pairs can go. With a purple button-down, a black wool sweater, and modern loafers, you'll fit right in at even the chicest spot.

TRAVEL DRESSY

Shhh. These jeans have a little bit of stretch woven into their fabric. Not so you can wear them tight, but so you can wear them comfortably. Pair them with a button-down and lightweight sweater.

TRAVEL CASUAL

These jeans with stretch have been washed for softness, but they'll still move with you without stretching out. Add a windbreaker and basketball shoes, and you may be mistaken for a pro athlete.

JEANS ARE MORE DOWNTOWN THAN COW TOWN, SO PAIR THEM WITH SOPHISTICATED FOOTWEAR THAT SHOWS YOUR STYLE. THERE'S A WORLD OF CHOICES AT YOUR FEET, FROM BOAT SHOES TO LOAFERS, BOOTS TO BUCKS.

WORKDAY
Bucks are an easy way to dress up denim for work. Note a signature sole adds a fun touch without being loud.

AFTER HOURS
This polished, slip-on loafer will give your going-out look an urban vibe.

WEEKEND
What's more American than canvas sneakers? They're great on men of all ages and style types, and work with every type of jeans.

TRAVEL
These sneakers combine the richness of suede with all the comfort of something you'd wear to the gym.

My significant other insisted I relegate my faded jeans to the back of my closet, but lately I've seen some pretty beat-up, washed-out pairs in stores and on billboards. Which is more current, dark-wash or light?

Old jeans never die, they just fade away. We'll always have a place in our heart for faded jeans, but for now save them for chore time—even if they seem to be the look of the moment. These days, the smart money is on the sophisticated look of darker shades, which can be worn in most any situation.

I've heard the term "selvedge." What does it mean?

When a denim edge is finished off on the loom (instead of cut off), it's known as a selvedge finish. Selvedge marks the highest quality denims, and selvedge jeans only grow finer with age. After about six months of wear, expect them to whisker, fade, and don wrinkle marks that enhance their look. Note that selvedge denim tends to shrink easily, so make sure you keep extra fabric when hemming to allow for shrinkage.

My body is tough to fit—I always have my pants altered. I'm not sure I've ever had jeans that really fit. Can jeans be altered?

With all those rivets, bar tacks, and triple seams, jeans are constructed expressly to resist change—so tailoring them is an engineering challenge and often not worth it. With such a broad range of options in fit—not to mention a huge range of waist and inseam measurements—the key to finding your perfect jeans is to try on as many pairs as possible. The one area where there's always room for a tailor's improvement? Length. You don't have to sacrifice the weathered hem when you shorten jeans, either: A Nordstrom tailor can save and reattach them at the proper length.

Jeans seem to be able to go just about anywhere now. Is there any place where jeans would not be appropriate?

Some would argue that a pair of really good jeans trumps even a dressy pair of trousers—after all, if you've anted up more than $200, you are not exactly dressing down. Still, leave the denim at home for weddings, funerals, and visits to the White House. And if you're not sure whether jeans are appropriate for your office environment, chances are they're probably not. Stick to chinos on casual Fridays.

STYLE TIP:
If you can only buy one pair of jeans, go for a style in dark denim, with a narrow leg and a medium rise, a classic style that will take most men anywhere.

NEVER JUDGE A BOOK BY ITS COVER, RIGHT? BUT WRAP THE GREAT AMERICAN NOVEL IN A CRUMMY DUST JACKET AND NO ONE WILL READ IT. OUTERWEAR MATTERS. IT WARMS, PROTECTS, AND KEEPS YOU LOOKING GOOD, EVEN WHEN FACING THE ELEMENTS. YOU DESERVE TO STEP OUT IN SOMETHING MORE DIGNIFIED THAN THE SHELL FROM YOUR SKI JACKET. THIS CHAPTER WILL SHOW YOU HOW.

WHETHER YOU'RE CLIMBING K2 OR ASCENDING THE CORPORATE LADDER, THERE'S A PIECE OF OUTERWEAR UP TO THE JOB.

In recent years, it's become socially acceptable to top off pretty much any outfit with a performance jacket. And while there are some great ones out there—replete with hoods, technical fabrics, and a seemingly endless supply of pockets—nothing takes the dash away from a dressy look like a piece of logo-emblazoned nylon. Consistency cuts the other way, too: Just like you wouldn't wear deck shoes with a wool suit, you wouldn't pair a camel overcoat with track pants. Every man needs an outerwear wardrobe to suit his lifestyle—especially when that lifestyle looks very different midweek than it does on Saturday.

Once you're aware of all the options out there, buying outerwear can become an addiction. How's a man supposed to choose between the camel hair coat and the grey cashmere one? Or the baseball jacket and the leather bomber? The good news is, a good jacket's appeal is timeless, so you'll be able to wear it forever. So go ahead and stock up. Jackets are like shoes—who has just one pair?

WHAT MAN DOESN'T YEARN TO LOOK LIKE BOGEY IN HIS ICONIC *CASABLANCA* TRENCH? HE'S COOL, URBANE, AND CAPABLE OF HANDLING NOT JUST THE ELEMENTS, BUT ANYTHING ELSE THAT COMES HIS WAY. OR THINK OF JAMES DEAN IN HIS BIKER JACKET, OR TOM CRUISE IN HIS BOMBER. THESE GUYS WERE BUNDLED UP IN SIGNATURE STYLE. YOU CAN BE, TOO—IN ANY ONE OF THESE ICONIC JACKETS.

PEA COAT

This woolen style, usually in navy blue, has been keeping us cozy for two hundred years. Roomy enough to wear over layers with a double-breasted cut that suits guys of all ages, this coat is a classic whether executed in boiled wool, the finest cashmere, or even cotton for warmer climes.

LEATHER JACKET

The muscle car of outerwear, this indispensable item lets everyone know there's a rock star in the building. Try it with jeans on a casual weekend or with wool trousers for a night on the town.

HYBRID

A catch-all term for jackets that serve more than one purpose, "hybrid" might as well mean multi-functional. With details varying from smartphone pockets to convertible collars, hybrid jackets prove you can have it all—in one.

CAR COAT

Those MG ragtops weren't big on warmth. As necessity is the mother of invention, along with the convertible emerged the car coat. Simple and short for sitting—with an A-line shape, single-breasted closure, and length that hits around mid-thigh—it looks great at any speed.

PARKA

Born of arctic extremes, the parka is the epitome of form following function. Rugged, roomy, waterproof, and insulated, today's parka can be found well below five thousand feet.

ACTIVE

From zip-up track jackets to fleece-lined hoodies, many of the most popular options in casual outerwear come right off the playing field. Sport and style are now on the same team with products that perform.

BLOUSON

No longer for members only, this classic lightweight jacket—usually made of nylon—is ideal for mild, unpredictable weather. It's your go-to jacket for the warmer seasons.

TRENCH COAT

If there's one outerwear piece that can take you anywhere, it's the trench. Its light weight makes it easy to pack; its waterproof fabric works over multiple layers or even just a T-shirt. Hey, it worked for Sherlock Holmes ...

fabric

NYLON READS SPORTY. GORE-TEX INDICATES ADVENTURE. CASHMERE SAYS POLISHED. SHINY, RUGGED, OR RICH, THE STUFF OUTERWEAR IS MADE OF BROADCASTS A STRONG STATEMENT. BUT LOOKS AREN'T EVERYTHING—IT'S WORTH KNOWING WHAT THESE FABRICS DO BEST.

NYLON
First widely used to make parachutes during World War II, nylon is a lightweight, synthetic fabric that keeps moisture out and warmth in.

LEATHER
If leather feels like a second skin, that's because it is. Warm yet breathable, leather has a texture and durability that's hard to imitate.

QUILTED POLYESTER
Equally at home on the slopes and on the streets, a parka says you're outdoorsy and style-savvy, too. Quilting is your best defense against wind chill, wherever you are.

MICROFIBER
The elements haven't a chance against microfiber's ability to repel water, insulate, and wick—all while looking a tad more formal than an active parka.

COTTON
Warm weather is not cotton's only season. Tightly woven cotton ably sheds wind and rain, all the while breathing and staying crisp.

WOOL, CASHMERE
Wool may be famous for its sturdiness, but add cashmere or camel hair and you'll find it has a soft side, too.

MORE THAN ANY OTHER CATEGORY OF CASUAL CLOTHING, THE DETAILS ON OUTERWEAR ARE ABOUT FUNCTION AND UTILITY. WHEN A JACKET HAS SPECIAL FEATURES, YOU'LL ACTUALLY MAKE USE OF THEM.

BUTTON-OUT LINING

A quality coat is a wise investment; with a button-out lining, you're essentially getting two coats for the price of one.

BELTS

Found not only at the waist but also at the cuffs and even the neck, belts seal out frigid winds and provide stylish details.

REINFORCED-PLASTIC-ZIPPERED POCKET

Loaded with goggles, gloves, and power bars, the pockets of active outerwear work hard—and reinforced plastic zippers close the whole deal.

SHEARLING

The shearling collars on bomber jackets aren't just for looks: At thirty thousand feet it can be fifty below. Whether lining the collar, cuffs, or the complete inner shell, shearling also promises sheer comfort.

STAND-UP BUTTONED COLLAR
With a stand-up collar, you'll be up to your neck in warm protection, even if you forget your scarf. Wear it open for a less prepped-out look.

RACING COLLAR
Steve McQueen wore a racing jacket with style. You too can zip up, strap that collar, and look danger squarely in the eye.

GROMMETS AND AIR VENTS
Don't sweat it—high-performance guys produce some non-atmospheric moisture. Performance jackets are vented to keep you dry inside as well as out.

EPAULETS
A nod to the military background of so many jackets, epaulets signal their wearer's high-ranking style.

WORKDAY CASUAL

If you're looking to upgrade your look, go for the classic brown bomber. Leather seems to magically adjust to whatever level of warmth you need, and it's the perfect everyday option to complement jeans and a sweater.

WORKDAY DRESSY

Here's what to choose when it's too warm for an overcoat but too dressy for a windbreaker. A city coat over your favorite sweater-and-button-down combo works whether you make your commute on foot or behind the wheel.

AFTER HOURS CASUAL

Military-inspired coats are perfect for the urban dresser. This detailed, neutral-colored jacket looks great thrown on over pretty much anything, but especially a striped tee and jeans.

AFTER HOURS DRESSY

Velvet works well in the form of a blazer. Combined with a variety of textures, from a slubbed linen T-shirt to a crisp button-down, the statement blazer is your go-to piece for a night out.

TRAVEL CASUAL
A windbreaker is a staggeringly versatile traveling companion. Because it's ultra-lightweight yet warm, you can stuff it in a backpack or keep it on your back at almost any destination. Try it in khaki instead of black or navy for a sporty vibe.

WEEKEND DRESSY
The bit of extra fabric afforded by a blouson jacket means it's always an easy fit; its elasticized waistband means it won't ever look sloppy— a necessity on a weekend when you've got to hop from one family event to the next.

TRAVEL DRESSY
When looking for a jacket to take on a trip, versatility is key. Whether you wear this one or pack it, a neutral nylon jacket works for every occasion you'll encounter on a chilly voyage.

WEEKEND CASUAL
Enter the streamlined, military-inspired puffer, which won't weigh you down, whether you're throwing snowballs or working in the yard. When you're going to be outside on a cool day, there's nothing better than a down jacket.

How much room should I allow for when I shop for a jacket? I might choose to wear a shirt underneath, or a sweater, or sport coat, or all three.
Fit is where most outerwear purchases go wrong, usually because guys hedge their bets and err on the side of too large. Wear a sweater or sport coat (or ask the salesperson to pull one for you), when you go shopping for outerwear. When you put on a coat, your magnificent form should show through, not disappear under bolts of fabric. Shoulders and armholes should be comfortable and allow for mobility. A piece of outerwear should always extend beyond the bottom of a sport coat. Sleeves should cover your wrists, just grazing the base of your thumb.

I like everything about my trench coat but the belt. What the heck do I do with it?
That belt seems to be trouble, but take it away and a trench is not a trench. Don't get too thrown by your belt; remember, you're in command here. You can guide your belt through the back and side loops and let it dangle, or tie the ends loosely behind so the belt reaches just halfway around. Perhaps best of all, tie it loosely in front—that's the way Bogey handled it. (Oddly enough, few men seem to use the actual buckle.)

Which coats should be altered? Which shouldn't?
Something loose-fitting like a snowboard jacket won't benefit much from alterations, nor will down-filled outerwear. However, classic wool, cashmere, and camel hair coats can be altered, and considering the investment you'll be making, it's always worth checking with a Nordstrom tailor for the correct fit.

STYLE TIP:
Many a man has been confounded by the prospect of what to wear over a blazer on a chilly night. Try layering underneath your blazer, instead of on top of it, for warmth. A cashmere sweater—or even a hoodie—will keep you feeling cozy while looking hip.

AS A RULE, EVERYDAY CLOTHING IS FAIRLY LOW-MAINTENANCE AND REQUIRES EXPONENTIALLY LESS ATTENTION THAN TAILORED CLOTHING. THAT SAID, EVERY PIECE YOU ADD TO YOUR WARDROBE IS AN INVESTMENT AND SHOULD BE TREATED AS SUCH.

DRY-CLEANING

Always follow the instructions on a garment's care label. Does "dry clean only" really mean dry clean only, you ask? Why yes, it does! Don't try to outsmart your clothing's manufacturer—garments have been tested extensively for performance.

SHIRTS

Most casual shirts are wash-and-wear, meaning they're meant to be a bit rumpled and/or faded. If you choose to clean them professionally, request "laundry service." Since dry cleaners tend to err on the side of starch, be sure to request "no starch" or "light starch" so that they come out soft, not crisp.

For extra-dark colors, spring for "dry-cleaning," which will keep dyes from fading, instead of laundry service.

Your fancy embroidered shirts are special, so treat them as such. Details mean dry clean only, please.

PANTS

One-hundred-percent cotton chinos and jeans should usually be laundered, not dry-cleaned. Ironing is optional, but make sure you tell your dry cleaner whether you want a crease ironed in.

OUTERWEAR

Most outerwear items will need to be dry-cleaned. You may have heard that a down jacket can be "fluffed up" with a trip through the dryer, but I don't recommend you try this at home.

Leather and suede must be cleaned according to a specific process—your dry cleaner knows what to do.

WASHING AT HOME

If a garment is labeled "hand-wash," put it in a basin full of cool water dosed with a capful of gentle detergent and use your hands to agitate, paying special attention to places where the garment makes contact with your skin (such as the armholes). Dry flat on top of a towel on a flat surface so the item doesn't lose its shape.

Fine fabrics such as cashmere, silk, and linen do well when hand-washed, then shaped and laid out to dry flat on a clean towel.

It goes without saying that the key to successful machine washing is sorting like with like. Put whites with whites and darks with darks, and always use cool water to keep clothes from shrinking and colors from running or fading.

Jeans should be turned inside out for washing. Air-drying preserves fit and color; the machine tends to stretch out jeans more quickly.

DID YOU KNOW?
Even though many home economists swear by running dirty sneakers through the washer and dryer, all that heat and bouncing destroys the integrity of the shoes. You're much better off spot-treating stains with diluted dishwashing liquid and a toothbrush.

SIZING THINGS UP

Everyday dressing is easy with its simplified sizing system. Sportswear pieces are normally sized in letters, not numbers.

HOW TO MEASURE

When measuring, a soft tape, like tailors use, is most accurate. As a general rule, the number of inches measured will equal your size, when measured correctly. Be sure to measure next to your body, not over a layer of clothing. A Nordstrom tailor would be happy to assist you in finding your proper measurements.

Head   Measure around your head, placing the tape level above your brow ridges.

Neck   Measure around your neck at the level of your Adam's apple. Add .5" to this measurement for comfort.

Chest   With arms at sides, measure around your upper body under your armpits and over the fullest part of your chest and shoulder blades, keeping tape parallel to the floor.

Waist   Determine how high on your waist or hip you would like to wear your pants, and measure at this point. Keep the tape comfortably loose and measure around the full circumference of your torso.

Hips   Stand with heels together and measure around the fullest part of your hips.

Sleeve   With arm bent at 90 degrees, place hand on hip. Have someone measure the distance from the center back of your neck, across the shoulder to the elbow, then down to the wrist.

Inseam   Select a pair of pants that fits you well and lay it on a flat surface. Measure from the crotch seam down to the ankle hem.

SIZE CHART: MEN'S APPAREL (PROPORTIONED FOR MEN UP TO 6' 3" TALL)

	SMALL	MEDIUM	LARGE	X-LARGE	XX-LARGE
Neck	14-14.5"	15-15.5"	16-16.5"	17-17.5"	18-18.5"
Chest	34-36"	38-40"	42-44"	46-48"	50-52"
Waist	28-30"	32-34"	36-38"	40-42"	44-46"
Hip	34-36"	38-40"	42-44"	45.5-47"	48.5-50"
Sleeve - Short Height 5' 3" to 5' 7"	31-31.5"	32-32.5"	33-33.5"	34-34.5"	
Sleeve - Regular Height 5' 8" to 6' 0"	32.5-33"	33.5-34"	34.5-35"	35.5-36"	36.5-37"
Sleeve - Tall Height 6' 1" to 6' 3"		35-35.5"	36-36.5"	37-37.5"	38"

NORDSTROM SERVICES

ON-SITE TAILORING AND ALTERATIONS
Receive complimentary alterations on most full-price apparel items purchased in store or at nordstrom.com.

COMPLIMENTARY PERSONAL STYLISTS
A Nordstrom Personal Stylist can help you with everything from buying a gift to putting together an entire wardrobe—they'll even do your shopping for you. Best of all, it's free of charge. Simply ask for a Personal Stylist at your nearest Nordstrom.

BUY ONLINE, PICK UP IN STORE
Need it right away? Just go to nordstrom.com and choose from selected items that can be shipped to your door or picked up at your nearest Nordstrom store in about an hour (during business hours).

EXTENDED SIZES
Pants, jackets, dress shirts, shoes, and more—you'll find an outstanding selection of sizes to ensure an exceptional fit. Selected Nordstrom stores and at nordstrom.com.

CERTIFIED SHOE FITTERS
At Nordstrom, you'll find salespeople specially trained to ensure you receive a perfect fit. An array of selected brands is also available in extended sizes.

SHOESHINE STAND
Located in the Men's Shoes area. Selected stores.

MADE-TO-ORDER DRESS SHIRTS AND TIES
Nordstrom crafts their made-to-order John W. Nordstrom dress shirts and ties for a personalized fit. Each shirt is made from Egyptian Giza two-ply cotton and fits your individual measurements. Choose between three fits, as many as eighty-five fabrics, and 130 neck and sleeve combinations. Custom-made neckwear comes in an array of fabrics, patterns are masterfully matched, and the workmanship is signature Nordstrom. Selected stores.

MADE-TO-MEASURE SUITS
A custom-tailored suit is the ultimate investment in quality and style. You choose the fabric, style, and cut. A Nordstrom salesperson will take your measurements and have your suit made by Armani Collezioni, Burberry, Hart Schaffner & Marx, Hickey Freeman, Joseph Abboud, or Ermenegildo Zegna. Selected stores.

THREE WAYS TO SHOP

RING US
Call 1.800.933.3365;
for TTY service for the deaf and
hard of hearing, call 1.800.685.2100.

CLICK HERE
Shop online 24/7
at nordstrom.com.

STOP BY
Simply visit your favorite
Nordstrom store.